I0147234

Today ...

MY FAVORITE DAY

A Journal Where the Grateful Grow

by
Susan O'Daniel

Dedicated to my husband who lovingly

supports me in all I hope to ever become

and lives passionately by my side.

For him, I am eternally grateful.

Published by

TBA *now*
think · believe · achieve

ISBN 978-0-9828724-0-6
© Copyright 2010

All rights reserved. No part of this book may be reproduced in any form,
except for brief reviews, without the written permission of the publisher.

TABLE OF
Contents

MY MEMORABLE ENTRIES

Today is _____ p. ____

Today is _____ p. ____

Today is _____ p. ____

Today is _____ p. ____

Today is _____ p. ____

Today is _____ p. ____

Today is _____ p. ____

Today is _____ p. ____

Today is _____ p. ____

Today is _____ p. ____

Today is _____ p. ____

Today is _____ p. ____

Today is _____ p. ____

Today is _____ p. ____

Today is _____ p. ____

Today is _____ p. ____

Today is _____ p. ____

Today is _____ p. ____

Today is _____ p. ____

Today is _____ p. ____

Today is _____ p. ____

Today is _____ p. ____

Today is _____ p. ____

Today is _____ p. ____

Today is _____ p. ____

Today is _____ p. ____

Today is _____ p. ____

Today is _____ p. ____

Today is _____ p. ____

AN INTRODUCTION TO

Gratefulness

What has been the most pivotal day of your life? Can you think of one day in which you were forever changed? If so, recall for a moment the event that caused your day to become so deeply significant, and think about the transformation that occurred in you. Did this life-changing event result in your *favorite* day?

For me, the day was December 10, 1987. On that day, my life changed forever. A horrific car accident left me with multiple, serious injuries including nine broken bones. A helicopter carried me to a hospital in Phoenix, and I remained in critical care for four days, unaware of all of the actions being taken to save my life. A lengthy hospital stay and a long recovery period followed. Nonetheless, this experience led to my favorite day.

You're probably wondering why on earth I would say a tragedy like this led to my favorite day. Let me explain. December 10, 1987, was pivotal. This day was the beginning of a journey through which I gained understanding and deep appreciation for my life. From that event forward, I grew tremendously as I began to realize and put into practice the power of healing *my thoughts*.

After reading an inspirational book given to me as a gift during my hospital stay, I came to an important understanding:

> *Each day is truly a gift from God, and what a present!*
> *I can unwrap each day with energy, excitement, and hope*
> *by simply choosing to do so. The events that occur during*
> *a day are not as important as how I react to those events.*
> *Controlling my thoughts can help create the kind of day*
> *I wish to enjoy, and it is up to me to make it happen.*

Becoming grateful was my first step in this process. Gratefulness created the foundation for building positive thoughts, including that of a healthy body and spirit. Being grateful helped me control *what* I thought and *how* I thought about everything that happened. It helped me focus my mind in the direction of possibilities rather than limitations and proved a great benefit in building the life I desired, a life of great fullness.

You, too, can open the door to possibilities in your life by controlling your thoughts, and *you have total control over your thoughts*! No one can *make* you have a specific thought, and you can choose to change each thought at will. Although you cannot control everything that happens to you in life, you can always control how you react by controlling how you think about each event.

Begin this process by being grateful for the incredible blessings you have in your life each and every day. *But wait*, you say, *I just had a terrible day, and nothing happened for which I can be grateful.* Truly, no matter what events happen to you in any given day, you can choose to still find the good, see the beautiful, and be thankful. After all, being in a terrible car accident and breaking nine bones doesn't seem like something for which to be thankful. But, without this event, I may have missed this very rewarding journey of gratefulness and change. Often our biggest and best moments of growth come from our deepest moments of despair or pain; we just need to open our thoughts to the incredible possibilities.

December 10, 1987. On that day, my life changed forever as a car accident led me to my favorite day. What is that day? Undoubtedly, with all of its possibilities and blessings, my favorite day is today!

I am confident this journal will help you see the many things for which you can, and should, be grateful. The positive energy in gratefulness will provide a solid foundation for you, and with this strength and support, every today can become your favorite day too!

FOR WHAT SHOULD I BE
Grateful?
The Path to Great Fullness

Gratefulness is a very powerful tool to use as you journey toward fulfillment in your life. If while using this journal, you have trouble coming up with ideas, you can return here for some inspiration. Begin by being thankful for even the smallest things. Just like drops of rain add together to form a flood, the sum of being grateful for each of the small things in your life can become a flood of fullness.

Remember, too, to be thankful each day for all that you have previously taken for granted and all of the good things you haven't previously noticed. Start with the basics and list at least twenty items for which you are thankful each day. Soon you will see that there are at least twenty things for which to be thankful in any given moment.

- Are you alive today? Be thankful! This means you have opportunities all around you, especially the opportunity to make choices about your thoughts. Perhaps you've heard the saying: "Yesterday is history, and tomorrow is a mystery, but today is a gift; that's why they call it the present!" Be grateful for this powerful present!

- What about your health? Even if you are physically challenged, sick, or in pain, you are alive and have purpose. As long as you can control your thoughts, you can be grateful for being alive. Remember to be grateful for all of your abilities including your ability to think and feel.

A clear reminder of the power behind focusing on our abilities and purpose came when I witnessed a quadriplegic artist painting his artwork using only his mouth to hold his delicate paintbrush. His body was motionless, and I imagine his life was difficult, but his gratitude for his purpose and ability were clearly expressed through his impressive, beautiful paintings of the life and scenery around him. I walked away inspired by him and deeply grateful for our encounter.

- Think about the people in your life. Feel alone? You're not! There are people who love you and people who want to love you if you allow them to know you. Most importantly, God loves you! Write it down.

- If you are one of the fortunate who has loved ones around you physically and/or emotionally, be thankful! Love is the most powerful force in the world! List each person whom you love and/or who loves you. Be grateful for them every day. Remember your pets too!

- Be grateful for all positive memories! Even after the loss of a loved one, you can choose to remember and be grateful for all of the positive memories. Be grateful for the time you had with your loved ones even if you were not granted as much time as you wanted. Grieving is certainly an important step in healing, but even in your grief, you can choose to focus on the good memories and be thankful for each of them, which can help you heal.

- You have you! You are a special, unique individual with endless possibilities. If you're not reaching for those possibilities, begin now. You have greatness within you. Be thankful for all of the good inside of you. List your strengths and your positive attributes. If this is a struggle for you, it may be an indication that you're not giving yourself enough love. Begin now!

- Notice the simple things and the simple moments each day: flowers, stars, sun, clouds, beauty anywhere, air to breathe, food to eat, clothes to wear, animals, and a place to live. Write them down, and you'll begin to notice and appreciate them more.

- Be grateful for freedom and for all of the men and women who brought freedom to you. Remember, too, those willing to defend it for you, both past and present. Freedom is a precious gift offering you unlimited choices and opportunities. List some choices and opportunities you have right now and be thankful to have the freedom to do so. Be grateful, also, for past choices and opportunities as they brought you happiness or a chance to learn and grow. What might future choices offer you?

On some pages in this journal I offer possible ideas to get you started, but endless possibilities exist if you open your mind and let them in! When you do, you'll begin to recognize many new things for which to be grateful. Soon, your gratefulness will reveal that your life is more rewarding and more fulfilling.

You will find pages with numbered lines from one to twenty while others are just a clean slate on which you can express your gratefulness. Feel free to use these pages to "write" your gratitude, or you can get more creative. Maybe you want to draw your thanks or diagram it somehow.

You can go through this journal in any order you choose—front to back, back to front, or randomly. Feel like you need a blank page? Turn to any blank page and draw or write whatever expresses your gratitude. Again, there is no *right* way to do this. Just begin, and watch your world become brighter!

THE TIME AND PLACE FOR EXPRESSING
Gratefulness

Is there a proper time of day to express your thanks? What about the proper place to be grateful? Great news! **There is no proper way, place, or time!** When I first began recording my gratefulness, I often wrote a list of twenty things for which I was thankful on a scrap of paper between classes. When I got home, I would try to find time to transfer the list to my journal, but it didn't always happen. When you do use your journal, the following suggestions may prove helpful.

When you first begin, try this: find a very peaceful spot to return to each day. Maybe it's beneath a tree, in a comfortable rocking chair, on a floor mat near a window, or simply in your bed. Wherever it might be for you, find it. If possible, play some relaxing music (no lyrics). You can find "mood" music in stores or on-line. Find music that brings you an immediate sense of calm and use it while you express your gratitude in your journal.

As for time, expressing gratitude when you first wake up is one idea. This allows you the opportunity to begin your day with purpose. If you begin each day by focusing on the wonderful things in your life, you set your mind in a healthy, happy direction and open the doors for a day full of wonder and awe. You will now be looking for the positive and surely you will see it.

Another idea is to express your gratitude at night. Just before sleeping, why not play some relaxing music and focus on the good from the day? No matter the events of the day, be grateful for the opportunities and remind yourself that tomorrow is a clean slate just waiting for you to make your mark. By remembering the good things from the day, and by being grateful before bedtime, you can fall asleep in a positive state of mind.

Although morning and evening offer great opportunities, in reality, it is the act of being grateful that is so critical; it isn't where, when, or how you express it. Therefore, simply begin at any time of day and wherever you choose. Just begin *today*!

As the days, months, and years of expressing gratitude pass, you will begin to see how much your life changes. Change is the one constant in our lives; nothing ever stays the same. By accepting change, we can find great, new opportunities before us. Be sure to always remain thankful for the experiences and precious memories of the past, but then move forward, being grateful for future opportunities of growth.

So, why begin this journey of gratefulness? When you do, I am confident your life will shine brighter as you develop the habit of seeing the positive side of life and being grateful for it. Truly in life, what you see is what you get. In you, I see an incredible human being with untapped potential, and I am grateful for you! Are you grateful too?

Today is _____

The only way to have

a friend is to be one.

~ Ralph Waldo Emerson

Today is _____

One possible idea for today: Be thankful for each
person with whom you have contact today, for each
person offers you an opportunity to give of yourself.

1. _____
2. _____
3. _____
4. _____
5. _____
6. _____
7. _____
8. _____
9. _____
10. _____
11. _____
12. _____
13. _____
14. _____
15. _____
16. _____
17. _____
18. _____
19. _____
20. _____

You are today where your

thoughts have brought you;

you will be tomorrow where

your thoughts take you.

~ James Lane Allen

Today is _____

Focus on the good things today, so your thoughts
lead you to where you want to go.

_____

_____

_____

_____

_____

_____

_____

_____

_____

_____

_____

_____

_____

_____

_____

_____

_____

_____

_____

*He is a wise man who does
not grieve for the things
which he has not, but rejoices
for those which he has.*

- Epictetus

Today is _____

Focus on what you have and be grateful
each and every day!

Be glad of life because it

gives you the chance to

love, to work, to play, and

to look up at the stars.

~ Henry VanDyke

Today is _____

Today, with whatever it brings, is a beautiful day.
Some way, some how, it offers a tremendous amount of beauty.
Let's find it!

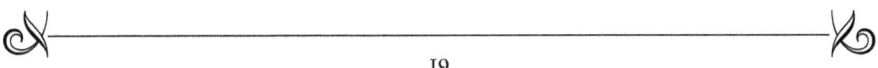

There is nothing
either good or bad, but
thinking makes it so.

~ Shakespeare, *Hamlet*

Today is _____

Think good thoughts and be glad for all of your blessings.

_____

_____

_____

_____

_____

_____

_____

_____

_____

_____

_____

_____

_____

_____

_____

_____

_____

_____

_____

_____

_____

_____

_____

Worry not what the future

has in store. Instead, take as a

gift whatever this day brings

to you and be thankful.

~ Susan O'Daniel

Today is _____

What gifts has this day offered?

Seven days without

thanks makes one weak.

~ Susan O'Daniel

Today is _____

For what are you thankful this day?

1. _____
2. _____
3. _____
4. _____
5. _____
6. _____
7. _____
8. _____
9. _____
10. _____
11. _____
12. _____
13. _____
14. _____
15. _____
16. _____
17. _____
18. _____
19. _____
20. _____

I awoke this morning with devout thanksgiving for my friends, the old and the new.

~ Ralph Waldo Emerson

Today is _____

Be grateful today for old friends, current friends,
and for those awaiting a future with you.

_____

_____

_____

_____

_____

_____

_____

_____

_____

_____

_____

_____

_____

_____

_____

_____

_____

_____

_____

_____

_____

_____

Life is an echo;

what you send out

comes back.

~ Chinese Proverb

Today is _____

Send out thanks today and watch it echo back!

As Ziggy once said,

You can complain because

roses have thorns,

or you can be grateful

because thorns have roses.

$\mathcal{T}\!oday$ is _____

Be grateful for having a choice in perspective and use it!

_____

_____

_____

_____

_____

_____

_____

_____

_____

_____

_____

_____

_____

_____

_____

_____

_____

_____

_____

_____

_____

Gratitude is riches.

Complaint is poverty.

~ Anonymous

Today is _____

What wealth you have this very moment! Be grateful!

1. _____
2. _____
3. _____
4. _____
5. _____
6. _____
7. _____
8. _____
9. _____
10. _____
11. _____
12. _____
13. _____
14. _____
15. _____
16. _____
17. _____
18. _____
19. _____
20. _____

A teacher affects eternity;

he can never tell where

his influence stops.

~ Henry Adams

$\mathcal{T}oday$ is _____

What teachings have you offered others today?
What teachings have been offered to you?

_____
_____
_____
_____
_____
_____
_____
_____
_____
_____
_____
_____
_____
_____
_____
_____
_____
_____
_____
_____
_____
_____

The best way to pay for a

lovely moment is to enjoy it.

- Richard Bach

Today is _____

Enjoy this moment right now, with whatever it holds,
and be grateful for it.

_____
_____
_____
_____
_____
_____
_____
_____
_____
_____
_____
_____
_____
_____
_____
_____
_____
_____
_____
_____
_____
_____
_____

You cannot always choose the situations you face in life, but you can always choose the attitudes to face those situations by monitoring your thoughts carefully.

~ Susan O'Daniel

Today is _____

Fear is a response;

courage is a decision.

Be courageous, and be

grateful for the decision.

~ Susan O'Daniel

Today is _____

_____
_____
_____
_____
_____
_____
_____
_____
_____
_____
_____
_____
_____
_____
_____
_____
_____
_____
_____
_____
_____
_____
_____

Keep your face to the

sunshine, and you will

not see the shadows.

- Helen Keller

Today is _____

Be grateful for all of the times you have seen the sunshine,
both literally and figuratively.

Abraham Lincoln once said,

People are about as

happy as they make up

their minds to be.

Today is _____

Make up your mind to be happy and grateful today.

_____
_____
_____
_____
_____
_____
_____
_____
_____
_____
_____
_____
_____
_____
_____
_____
_____
_____
_____
_____
_____
_____
_____
_____

*Improvement begins
with "I."*

*I am grateful today as
I am improving.*

~ Susan O'Daniel

Today is _____

I am grateful today for:

1. _____
2. _____
3. _____
4. _____
5. _____
6. _____
7. _____
8. _____
9. _____
10. _____
11. _____
12. _____
13. _____
14. _____
15. _____
16. _____
17. _____
18. _____
19. _____
20. _____

Whatever we think

about and thank about

we bring about.

~ Dr. John F. Demartini

Today is _____

What great things are you thinking about?
Be grateful for having a choice in how you think!

Opportunities are

usually disguised as hard

work, so most people

don't recognize them.

~ Ann Landers

Today is _____

What "opportunities" have you encountered today?
Be grateful for all of the good experience found
through hard work. Remember to be thankful for
the people who may have helped you.

_____

_____

_____

_____

_____

_____

_____

_____

_____

_____

_____

_____

_____

_____

_____

_____

_____

_____

_____

_____

_____

Remember, it is not in being loved *but* in loving *that we are blessed.*

~ Susan O'Daniel

Today is _____

Today, be grateful for love — past, present, and future.

1. _____
2. _____
3. _____
4. _____
5. _____
6. _____
7. _____
8. _____
9. _____
10. _____
11. _____
12. _____
13. _____
14. _____
15. _____
16. _____
17. _____
18. _____
19. _____
20. _____

"It's today!" squeaked Piglet.

"My favorite day," said Pooh.

~ From *The Tao of Pooh* by Benjamin Hoff

Today is _____

Why is today (and each and every day) your favorite day?

If you don't think
every day is a good one,
just try missing one.

~ Cavett Robert

Today is _____

What are you grateful for today?

1. _____
2. _____
3. _____
4. _____
5. _____
6. _____
7. _____
8. _____
9. _____
10. _____
11. _____
12. _____
13. _____
14. _____
15. _____
16. _____
17. _____
18. _____
19. _____
20. _____

What you get by achieving

your goals is not as important

as what you become by

achieving your goals.

- Zig Ziglar

Today is _____

What goals have you met?
Who have you become because of your achievements?

_____

_____

_____

_____

_____

_____

_____

_____

_____

_____

_____

_____

_____

_____

_____

_____

_____

_____

_____

_____

_____

A gentle reminder:

Learn to say a good goodbye

whether it's leaving the house each

morning or saying a final goodbye

to a loved one.

Be grateful for the time you

had together.

~ Susan O'Daniel

Today is _____

Life is what we make

of it, always has been,

always will be.

~ Grandma Moses

Today is _____

Think about this:
The smallest good deed is a great moment.
What good deeds did you do today?
What good deeds have been done for you today?

1. _____
2. _____
3. _____
4. _____
5. _____
6. _____
7. _____
8. _____
9. _____
10. _____
11. _____
12. _____
13. _____
14. _____
15. _____
16. _____
17. _____
18. _____
19. _____
20. _____

Trust me on this: The more you are thankful, the more you will have for which to be thankful.

~ Susan O'Daniel

Today is _____

_____
_____
_____
_____
_____
_____
_____
_____
_____
_____
_____
_____
_____
_____
_____
_____
_____
_____
_____
_____
_____
_____

Time is our most valuable asset, yet we tend to waste it, kill it, spend it, and not invest it.

- Jim Rohn

Today is _____

In what good ways have you invested your time?

1. _____
2. _____
3. _____
4. _____
5. _____
6. _____
7. _____
8. _____
9. _____
10. _____
11. _____
12. _____
13. _____
14. _____
15. _____
16. _____
17. _____
18. _____
19. _____
20. _____

*You can have anything
you want in life if you just
help enough other people
get what they want.*

- Zig Ziglar

Today is _____

How have you helped others today? What are some specific
things you can do to help others today or tomorrow?
Commit to doing them!

Kind words can be
short and easy to
speak, but their echoes
are truly endless.

- Mother Teresa

$\mathcal{T}\!oday$ is _____

When have kind words made a positive impact on you?
Be grateful. If possible, you might want to share the impact it
made with the person who said the words.
For today, make it a goal to speak kind words (honest and from
your heart) to people with whom you have contact.

_____

_____

_____

_____

_____

_____

_____

_____

_____

_____

_____

_____

_____

_____

_____

_____

_____

_____

_____

*When we take responsibility
for how we react to everything
in life, we empower ourselves
with choice, and we free
ourselves from being victims.*

~ Susan O'Daniel

Today is _____

> There is no room for blame in life.
> Find the good in everyone today.

He that cannot forgive others

breaks the bridge over which

he, himself, must pass.

- Lord Herbert

Be grateful that you have been forgiven and be grateful
for the choice to forgive others. Forgiveness does not
excuse the actions of another, but it frees you from the
bondage and pain of hanging on to the resentment.
Forgiving others, as well as yourself, is truly a blessing.

_____

_____

_____

_____

_____

_____

_____

_____

_____

_____

_____

_____

_____

_____

_____

_____

_____

_____

We must become the change

we wish to see in the world.

~ Mahatma Gandhi

Today is _____

Be grateful, today, for the lessons in your life that are helping to
create the person you are becoming. For what can you
be grateful today? Gratefulness helps begin the process of
change in a positive direction.

_____

_____

_____

_____

_____

_____

_____

_____

_____

_____

_____

_____

_____

_____

_____

_____

_____

_____

_____

_____

_____

It is better to light

the candle than to

curse the darkness.

~ Eleanor Roosevelt

Today is _____

Today, list the things for which you are grateful.
Find positives in even the rough spots of the day.

1. _____
2. _____
3. _____
4. _____
5. _____
6. _____
7. _____
8. _____
9. _____
10. _____
11. _____
12. _____
13. _____
14. _____
15. _____
16. _____
17. _____
18. _____
19. _____
20. _____

Take in the fullness of each day

as no one is promised tomorrow.

~ Susan O'Daniel

Today is _____

How will you fill your day today?

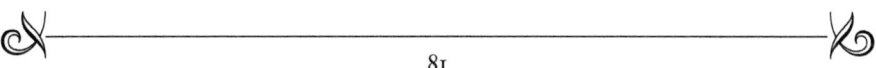

*Happiness is not having
what you want.*

*Happiness is wanting
what you have.*

~ Rabbi Hyman Schachtel

Today is _____

Remember to be grateful for what you have today.

_____
_____
_____
_____
_____
_____
_____
_____
_____
_____
_____
_____
_____
_____
_____
_____
_____
_____
_____
_____
_____
_____
_____
_____
_____

What lies behind us,

and what lies before us,

are tiny matters compared

to what lies within us.

~ William Morrow

Today is _____

Think about the good person within you.
Admire your great qualities and be grateful for how
these qualities were formed within you.

1. _____
2. _____
3. _____
4. _____
5. _____
6. _____
7. _____
8. _____
9. _____
10. _____
11. _____
12. _____
13. _____
14. _____
15. _____
16. _____
17. _____
18. _____
19. _____
20. _____

Time flies.

It's up to you to

be the navigator.

~ Robert Orben

Today is _____

Be grateful for this moment. Navigate well!
What situations have you navigated well today?
How did your choices help others as well as you?

_____
_____
_____
_____
_____
_____
_____
_____
_____
_____
_____
_____
_____
_____
_____
_____
_____
_____
_____
_____
_____

Failure is simply an opportunity to begin more intelligently.

~ Henry Ford

Today is _____

What lessons have you learned by beginning again? Remind
yourself of the good lessons and the growth you have made.

*If today were your
last day, would you be
wishing it to be over?*

~ Susan O'Daniel

Today is _____

> Slow down today, take in each precious moment,
> and be grateful.

Well done is

better than well said.

- Benjamin Franklin

Today is _____

There are many things each day that you do well, but most of us take them for granted. Today, credit yourself for the things you have done well. Don't forget the small stuff. Added together, the small stuff becomes big stuff.

1. _____

2. _____

3. _____

4. _____

5. _____

6. _____

7. _____

8. _____

9. _____

10. _____

11. _____

12. _____

13. _____

14. _____

15. _____

16. _____

17. _____

18. _____

19. _____

20. _____

If we could see the miracle of
a single flower clearly, our
whole life would change.

~ Buddha

Today is _____

Enjoy the scenery of the day!
This day is only here this one time.

_____
_____
_____
_____
_____
_____
_____
_____
_____
_____
_____
_____
_____
_____
_____
_____
_____
_____
_____
_____
_____
_____
_____
_____
_____

A smooth sea never

made a skilled mariner.

~ English proverb

Today is _____

What skills are you developing each day
through the trials set before you?
Be grateful for the opportunities to develop those skills.

1. _____
2. _____
3. _____
4. _____
5. _____
6. _____
7. _____
8. _____
9. _____
10. _____
11. _____
12. _____
13. _____
14. _____
15. _____
16. _____
17. _____
18. _____
19. _____
20. _____

I wept because I had

no shoes, until I saw a

man who had no feet.

~ Ancient Persian saying

Today is _____

Be grateful for all you have.

Never to suffer

would have been never

to have been blessed.

~ Edgar Allan Poe

Today is _____

Find and count your blessings today!

_____
_____
_____
_____
_____
_____
_____
_____
_____
_____
_____
_____
_____
_____
_____
_____
_____
_____
_____
_____
_____
_____
_____
_____
_____

Everything has its beauty,

but not everyone sees it.

~ Confucius

Today is _____

Find the beauty in everything!

*Courage is not the
lack of fear. It is
acting in spite of it.*

~ Mark Twain

Today is _____

Be thankful for even those things you fear acting upon.
They offer you a marvelous opportunity
to stretch your comfort zone!

1. _____
2. _____
3. _____
4. _____
5. _____
6. _____
7. _____
8. _____
9. _____
10. _____
11. _____
12. _____
13. _____
14. _____
15. _____
16. _____
17. _____
18. _____
19. _____
20. _____

*A happy person is not a
person in a certain set of
circumstances, but rather
a person with a certain
set of attitudes.*

~ William Morrow

Today is _____

Look at all of the circumstances you will face today or
have faced today, and examine your attitudes about them.
Write about the positive attitudes you embrace.

_____

_____

_____

_____

_____

_____

_____

_____

_____

_____

_____

_____

_____

_____

_____

_____

_____

_____

_____

_____

_____

_____

*It never hurts your
eyesight to look on the
bright side of things.*

~ Anonymous

Today is _____

See the bright side now. Find it!
There is a bright side to every circumstance
if we are just willing to see it.

Don't wait for great

opportunities.

Seize common, everyday

ones and make them great.

~ Napoleon Hill

Today is _____

What opportunities, no matter how small, can you make great?
For instance, can you bring a smile to a stranger's face?
This small gesture may change someone's day
or even someone's life. Maybe it is just what he or she needs
right now in order to see hope.

_____

_____

_____

_____

_____

_____

_____

_____

_____

_____

_____

_____

_____

_____

_____

_____

_____

_____

_____

Learn from yesterday,

live for today,

hope for tomorrow.

- Anonymous

Today is _____

_____

_____

_____

_____

_____

_____

_____

_____

_____

_____

_____

_____

_____

_____

_____

_____

_____

_____

_____

_____

_____

_____

_____

_____

*Ability is what you're
capable of doing.*

*Motivation determines
what you do.*

*Attitude determines
how well you do it.*

~ Lou Holtz

Today is _____

Be grateful today for your abilities
including your ability to be grateful.

*Argue for your
limitations, and sure
enough, they're yours.*

~ Richard Bach

Today is _____

Today, let's look at all of the possibilities
and forget the limitations.
I am grateful for the possibility of reaching <u>you</u> today.

_____
_____
_____
_____
_____
_____
_____
_____
_____
_____
_____
_____
_____
_____
_____
_____
_____
_____
_____
_____

Life is one grand,

sweet song,

so start the music.

~ Ronald Reagan

Today is _____

      Be grateful today for life and all it offers.

Unless you try to do

something beyond what you

have already mastered

you will never grow.

- Ronald E. Osborn

Today is _____

Be grateful, today, for all of your growth until now.
Then, commit to growing more – today!

1. _____
2. _____
3. _____
4. _____
5. _____
6. _____
7. _____
8. _____
9. _____
10. _____
11. _____
12. _____
13. _____
14. _____
15. _____
16. _____
17. _____
18. _____
19. _____
20. _____

I have not failed;

I have just found 10,000

ways that won't work.

~ Thomas Edison, after trying
   an experiment 10,000 times

Today is _____

Be grateful for your success even when it does not
appear to be the "success" you envisioned.

_____

_____

_____

_____

_____

_____

_____

_____

_____

_____

_____

_____

_____

_____

_____

_____

_____

_____

_____

_____

Your chances of success

in any undertaking can

always be measured by

your belief in yourself.

~ Robert Collier

Today is _____

Gratefulness can help you see and appreciate all of the good in your life, which can, in turn, help you gain belief in yourself.

1. _____
2. _____
3. _____
4. _____
5. _____
6. _____
7. _____
8. _____
9. _____
10. _____
11. _____
12. _____
13. _____
14. _____
15. _____
16. _____
17. _____
18. _____
19. _____
20. _____

In just two days,

tomorrow will be yesterday.

~ Susan O'Daniel

Today is _____

Live fully each day and be thankful for it!

Making choices is self-empowering.
Recognize all the opportunities
for choice in your life and become
someone who acts rather than
simply reacts.

~ Susan O'Daniel

Today is _____

Be thankful for choice!

*A thankful heart is not only
the greatest virtue, but the
parent of all other virtues.*

~ Marcus Tullius Cicero

Today is _____

Reminder:
Being full of thanks each and every day helps form a
healthy, positive attitude.

1. _____
2. _____
3. _____
4. _____
5. _____
6. _____
7. _____
8. _____
9. _____
10. _____
11. _____
12. _____
13. _____
14. _____
15. _____
16. _____
17. _____
18. _____
19. _____
20. _____

There are only two ways

to live your life.

One is as though

nothing is a miracle.

The other is as though

everything is a miracle.

~ Albert Einstein

Today is _____

What miracles happened today? Be thankful.

1. _____
2. _____
3. _____
4. _____
5. _____
6. _____
7. _____
8. _____
9. _____
10. _____
11. _____
12. _____
13. _____
14. _____
15. _____
16. _____
17. _____
18. _____
19. _____
20. _____

Democracy does not guarantee

equality of conditions;

it only guarantees

equality of opportunity.

~ Susan O'Daniel

Today is _____

What wonderful opportunities did you find today?

_____

_____

_____

_____

_____

_____

_____

_____

_____

_____

_____

_____

_____

_____

_____

_____

_____

_____

_____

_____

_____

_____

_____

_____

The strongest principle of
growth lies in human choice.

~ George Eliot

Today is _____

Be grateful for every chance to learn and grow.

A person will be called to account on Judgment Day for every permissible thing he might have enjoyed but did not.

- The Talmud

Today is _____

Enjoy all that life has to offer!

1. _____
2. _____
3. _____
4. _____
5. _____
6. _____
7. _____
8. _____
9. _____
10. _____
11. _____
12. _____
13. _____
14. _____
15. _____
16. _____
17. _____
18. _____
19. _____
20. _____

The last of human freedoms –

to choose one's attitude in any

given set of circumstances, to

choose one's own way.

~ Victor Frankl

Today is _____

Attitude is a little thing
that makes a big difference in all of life.

_____
_____
_____
_____
_____
_____
_____
_____
_____
_____
_____
_____
_____
_____
_____
_____
_____
_____
_____
_____
_____
_____

Regardless of your lot
in life, you can build
something beautiful on it.

~ Zig Ziglar

Today is _____

What beauty have you built in your life
regardless of good or bad circumstances?

Develop the happiness habit,

and life will become

a continual feast.

~ Norman Vincent Peale

Today is _____

Habits are formed through repetition.
Make gratefulness a habit and
happiness is sure to stand beside it.

_____
_____
_____
_____
_____
_____
_____
_____
_____
_____
_____
_____
_____
_____
_____
_____
_____
_____
_____
_____

I bring you the gift of

these four words:

I believe in you.

~ Blaise Pascal

Today is _____

To whom do you give your support?
Whose support do you enjoy? Be sure to give them thanks.

1. _____
2. _____
3. _____
4. _____
5. _____
6. _____
7. _____
8. _____
9. _____
10. _____
11. _____
12. _____
13. _____
14. _____
15. _____
16. _____
17. _____
18. _____
19. _____
20. _____

*If you want to stand
out, don't be different,
be outstanding.*

~ Anonymous

Today is _____

In what ways are you outstanding?

It is always

your next move.

~ Napoleon Hill

Today is _____

Be grateful for the choice you have in your next
move, and the next, and the next!

1. _____
2. _____
3. _____
4. _____
5. _____
6. _____
7. _____
8. _____
9. _____
10. _____
11. _____
12. _____
13. _____
14. _____
15. _____
16. _____
17. _____
18. _____
19. _____
20. _____

The work of the individual still remains the spark that moves mankind ahead.

~ Igor I. Sikorsky

Today is _____

Be grateful for the opportunities you
have had, and still have, to contribute to mankind.

_____

_____

_____

_____

_____

_____

_____

_____

_____

_____

_____

_____

_____

_____

_____

_____

_____

_____

_____

_____

_____

_____

Every problem has a

gift for you in its hands.

~ Richard Bach

Today is _____

What gifts have you received from problems?
The gifts are there; find them!

1. _____
2. _____
3. _____
4. _____
5. _____
6. _____
7. _____
8. _____
9. _____
10. _____
11. _____
12. _____
13. _____
14. _____
15. _____
16. _____
17. _____
18. _____
19. _____
20. _____

*Opportunity often
comes disguised in the
form of misfortune,
or temporary defeat.*

~ Napoleon Hill

Today is _____

What healthy opportunities do you see before you?
Take them!

_____
_____
_____
_____
_____
_____
_____
_____
_____
_____
_____
_____
_____
_____
_____
_____
_____
_____
_____
_____
_____
_____

*Life is short, and it's up
to you to make it sweet.*

~ Sarah Delany

Today is _____

Remember to count each blessing
beginning with the blessing of today.

1. _____

2. _____

3. _____

4. _____

5. _____

6. _____

7. _____

8. _____

9. _____

10. _____

11. _____

12. _____

13. _____

14. _____

15. _____

16. _____

17. _____

18. _____

19. _____

20. _____

Learning is not compulsory.

Neither is survival.

~ W. Edwards Deming

Today is _____

What have you learned today? Don't forget the
small lessons as they, too, are important.

An optimist laughs to forget.

A pessimist forgets to laugh.

~ Anonymous

Today is _____

Be grateful for the joy of laughter
and set a goal to laugh more often.
List the 20 things for which you are grateful today.

1. _____
2. _____
3. _____
4. _____
5. _____
6. _____
7. _____
8. _____
9. _____
10. _____
11. _____
12. _____
13. _____
14. _____
15. _____
16. _____
17. _____
18. _____
19. _____
20. _____

Think of every thought as a seed.

If you plant weeds, you can't

expect flowers to grow.

How is your garden growing?

~ Susan O'Daniel

Today is _____

What positive seeds did you plant today?

You'll always miss

100% of the shots

you don't take.

~ Wayne Gretsky

Today is _____

Be grateful for your "shots on goal." When shots
become available, commit to taking them.

1. _____
2. _____
3. _____
4. _____
5. _____
6. _____
7. _____
8. _____
9. _____
10. _____
11. _____
12. _____
13. _____
14. _____
15. _____
16. _____
17. _____
18. _____
19. _____
20. _____

Nothing lasts forever,

not even your troubles.

~ A. Glasgow

Today is _____

Even if you're on the

right track, you'll get run

over if you just sit there.

~ Will Rogers

Today is _____

> Movement can be both physical and mental,
> and both types of movement are important.
> Change happens, so encourage change in the direction
> you desire by moving in that direction starting today.

We are what we

repeatedly do.

Excellence then, is not

an act but a habit.

~ Aristotle

Today is _____

What good things do you repeatedly do?

Ever feel like you're going nowhere? Look at nowhere this way: you are simply now here.

~ Susan O'Daniel

$\mathcal{T}$*oday* is _____

Where do you want to go from here?
Be grateful, again, for choice!

_____
_____
_____
_____
_____
_____
_____
_____
_____
_____
_____
_____
_____
_____
_____
_____
_____
_____
_____
_____
_____
_____
_____
_____

*A journey of a
thousand miles begins
with a single step.*

~ Chinese Proverb

Today is _____

Congratulate yourself for taking a step into gratefulness!
It is a journey worth continuing.

My thanksgiving is perpetual ...

O how I laugh when I think of

my vague indefinite riches.

No run on my bank can drain it

for my wealth is not possession

but enjoyment.

~ Henry David Thoreau

www.ingramcontent.com/pod-product-compliance
Lightning Source LLC
Chambersburg PA
CBHW052044090426
42739CB00010B/2045